MINIMALIST AND LUXURY
LIVING SPACES

Fashionable Home Design

Edited by Mark Rielly

images
Publishing

CONTENTS

FOREWORD

by Mark Rielly, ARRCC Director

'Less is more' is a phrase adopted by one of the founders of modern design, architect Mies van der Rohe, as a guiding principal for minimalist design. As a movement, minimalism has looked to strip away ornamentation and detail, rejecting the lavish and opulent layering of highly decorative styles of the past.

Defined as a period of design in the 1960s and 1970s, the origin of this design style however can be traced to the simple and abstract ideas of the De Stijl, 'the style' in Dutch, an artistic movement active from 1917 to the 1930s. Although this movement did not last very long, it laid the foundation for minimalism as a design style. On a practical level, it advocated simple visual compositions and the use of black and white together with primary colors. Traditional Japanese design is seen as another predecessor to minimalism due to its simplicity and clean forms.

In broad terms, minimalist design can be defined as a style of simplicity, stripping away all that is superfluous and incorporating only functional and necessary elements in the design. The emphasis on simplicity is carried through to the choice and use of materials and limited colour palettes. The style can be described as focusing on the design elements that need to be there without layering and embellishment. This 'design for purpose' is often seen as too functional, stark and cold, a white box or an ultra-modern interior, but minimalism is not about complete lack of decoration, but rather the select choice of elements and finishes that symbolize the ultimate in luxurious living.

Minimalist interiors are seen as serene sanctuaries where subdued hues and palettes inspire a sense of calm; the spaces are emotive and tell a simple story. The design narrative fully incorporates order, proportion, and light, balancing function and aesthetics.

Mies van der Rohe's Barcelona Pavilion, designed for the 1929 International Exposition, stands out as an iconic example of minimalist design and is an expression of extreme simplicity. Simple horizontal and vertical planes intersect and are perfectly balanced to create spaces that are solid and void, framing Zen-like moments. Natural lighting migrating through the spaces is elegantly captured, enhancing the extravagant use of materials and finishes, such as onyx and marble. Together with the Pavilion design, Mies also created simple furniture specifically for the building, including the famous Barcelona chair.

The expression of minimalist design varies significantly and the contrast can be seen in the spartan designs of architects like Tadao Ando and John Pawson to the more sophisticated and luxurious minimalist interiors by designers such as Vincent Van Duysen and Joseph Dirand. Where Ando and Pawson's work are more rooted in Japanese Zen moments reducing everything to a bare minimum, Duysen and Dirand create interiors with a more curated approach to luxurious design. What is evident through their work and design methodology is that each design consideration has a purpose where its aesthetic value is absorbed, creating a timeless design.

Minimalism has influenced all spheres of design including art, fashion, branding, and, now, the way we live. With the information overload in today's technological world, minimalism has also become a way of life and a philosophy to living higher quality experiences. Minimalists consciously live a life with only the essentials and have turned their backs on everything else.

Today's minimalist interiors respond to the modern urge to purge. Living in a world where marketing and advertising sell the temptation to accumulate, the desire for a more simplistic life stems from the need to slow down. With a more conscious approach towards how we wish to live, the need for space to breathe and energize, to take rest and disconnect has influenced design. Interior spaces are conceptualized without superfluous elements to give visual impact with an emphasis on the aesthetic value. The intuitive need to live more simplistic lives has led to the symbolic exploration of the environments in which we live and how we design them. Creating interiors that are more meaningful and long-lasting within a distinctive vision. Minimalist interiors are more serene, where simplicity creates a more relaxed environment in which to enjoy the rituals and basic pleasures of everyday living.

As minimalist designers, we strive to express the language of simplicity. At ARRCC, we believe in detailed minimalism, using raw, organic materials with shape and form. This often results in layered interiors that add richness to the minimalistic design. Soft curves

within rigid structures, ordinary materials used in extraordinary ways — these are all areas in which we add our signature to minimalist designs. In minimalist design, color is also expressed in a simple form. Color is either emphasized with extremely limited palettes in single hues or strikingly contrasted to create a balanced extreme.

Where minimalistic design is interpreted as luxury design, we still find within this approach a simplicity in concept, incorporating the principles of functional design in simplified ways where clean lines in architecture, subtlety of light, and calming tones embrace glamour, comfort and sophistication. Even though minimalism strips away ornamentation and detail, the design can still be rich and layered. The ability to strike a balance between minimalism and luxury is a carefully considered harmonious application of concepts distinguished by the application of superior finishes.

Through the simplification of interior spaces, the style creates a sense of definition focused on the richness of simplicity, giving a heightened awareness of space. Through the use of rich materials and a distinctive play on lighting, minimalist interiors can maintain a sense of spatial complexity and, even though simple in appearance, they surprise.

With the use of exotic materials and high cost associated with simplistic detailing, Minimalist design is very often seen as expensive and has resulted in the connotation that minimalism is a luxury, but this should not be confused with the vision and sensibility of minimalist design. Luxury is defined as a state of comfort involving great expense, but in minimalist design, the luxury is not in the expense of the detail but rather the experience of the detail.

Minimalism at its best requires perfection and interiors seen as flawlessly executed—a careful curation of selected materials together with considered placement of interior furnishings.

Not often do you find a book that has so well captured every facet of minimalist design. Reviewing this book, I was struck by the diverse design languages used, from the simple lines of GRAY BOX, an incredible design by AD Architecture, to the spectacular HAUS K created by destilat in Austria. The book is beautifully illustrated and features over 30 projects, filled with pages of inspiringinteriors from a variety of places from around the globe, including China, Spain, Germany, Italy, the United States, Greece, The Netherlands, Switzerland, Canada, Austria, Ukraine, Israel, and France. The

locations in this publication cover a diverse range of projects, from city apartments to country villas.

The interiors presented here offer new takes on minimalism and luxury with designs that are original, interesting, and daring. Each project captures a distinctive approach transcending trends. These interiors stand out from the hustle and bustle of everyday life, providing serene havens, imagined and created by diversely talented architects and designers.

Each project is uniquely different capturing a snapshot of those who live in these homes and the expression of simplistic design encapsulated in the architecture, interiors ,and decoration of minimalism.

If you are looking for design inspiration, the collection of projects captured here are a rich reservoir of ideas showcasing inspiring rooms filled with unique furniture and art pieces to covet. This collection of projects and designers creates a unique opportunity to compare the varied approaches to minimalist design all in one volume.

Mark Rielly's profile

Mark Rielly is a renowned South African interior architect, known for creating rich, layered residential and leisure interiors across the globe. After studying architecture and working at SAOTA as a Project Architect for a number of years, his passion for interior design and for conceptualizing and articulating interior spaces, led to the creation of ARRCC interior design studio. Under his creative design leadership, ARRCC has gained a reputation as a growing international brand, creating some of the most exclusive interiors in London, New York, Paris, Moscow, Miami, Dubai, Ibiza, Geneva, Dakar, Sydney, Shenzhen, and more.

Mark's passion for art and design, coupled with his relentless pursuit of perfection, is at the core of his successful career. He inspires those around him and leads them to create exceptional, award-winning interiors that capture a design language and an aesthetic distinctively dynamic and surpassing trends.

CASE STUDIES

ALTA CHALET

Alta Chalet is designed as a year-round weekend retreat for a family of five, comprising 3000 square feet (280 square meters) of efficiently planned living space spread over two storys.

The inversion of program results in the public spaces occupying the top floor to facilitate appreciation of long vistas to the surrounding ski hills. Here, the family congregates in the open-concept kitchen, dining and living areas; a private den with access to a large south-facing outdoor deck completes the arrangement. Below, the ground floor comprises more intimate functions of a bed and bath, along with a sauna and direct access to the outdoor hot tub deck. A garage accommodates two vehicles, with extra room for storing skis and other recreational equipment. Notably, primary access to the chalet is neatly concealed, mediated through a screened and covered entry passage articulated with vertically oriented wood slats painted white. This device achieves not only privacy and protection from the elements, but also a diffusely lit transitionary sequence for those arriving and departing.

In the interior, the spare qualities of the exterior are reflected through an understated but refined material palette: every aspect is meticulously detailed. Walls and sloped ceiling planes form a sculptural composition in matte white that amplifies winter light and the purity of the snow outside, enhancing the expression of light and shadow throughout the course of the day. Wide-plank oak floors and rift-cut white oak millwork convey warmth and tactility. The drama of the blackened steel fireplace establishes a focal point in the main living area; its threshold demarcated by a pleasingly textured flamed basalt hearth.

With sustainability at the forefront of the design process, the requirement of material durability and longevity was paramount. Thus, low-maintenance prefinished Canadian pine siding and a high-performance metal roof were specified for the building exterior. To reduce the ecological footprint further, energy consumption was decreased through a high-performance glazing system, hydronic radiant in-floor heating, additional insulation and a wood-burning fireplace. Natural lighting and ventilation was optimized through the provision of several large, operable windows.

Alta Chalet establishes a legacy of a hybrid housing prototype, inspired by the long-standing tradition of agrarian architecture. Combining the practical utility required of contemporary life with the dignified stoicism of traditional barn structures, the project aspires to re-evaluate the role of the typical suburban home and assign it architectural validity through a rigorous deconstruction and thoughtful recalibration.

Location | Blue Mountains, Ontario, Canada **Area** | 3000 square feet (280 square meters) **Completion** | 2015
Design | AKB Architects **Photography** | Shai Gil, Bob Gundu

View of living, dining, and kitchen area

Kitchen

Master bedroom

Bathroom vanity

ARA # 56 HOUSE

Redesigning a house with practically the same layout but with a totally different spatial conception is always a desirable challenge for an architect, since the raw material to work with are space and light. Having the best raw material available, for clients who appreciates these tools, helps guarantees success.

Spatially, the house had to have large open spaces and possibilities to connect with others to become even bigger. The house worked with an open plan, where the arrangement of architectural elements as well as furniture, both fixed and movable, never finish closing the space. Instead, they are arranged so that they order the visuals, thus providing in an immaterial way the character of section of the house.

To achieve this, the design defined OX architecture when dealing with the functional problems of the interior, designing specific elements of furniture to solve particular functional problems.

On the ground floor, two problems had to be solved. The first consisted in placing an element of separation, exclusively of visuals, between the main entrance to the house and the main living room and the living area linked to the kitchen. The design of a white latticework with 0.12-inch (3-millimeter) Z-shaped folded steel vertical elements allowed the light entering through the large south-facing windows to be sifted through it, causing the entrance to be connected to the exterior while controlling visual intimacy. The Z-shape of the vertical pieces and the curved arrangement of the whole set, influences the idea that manages the whole house. The effects of natural and artificial light make it the fundamental point that articulates the house.

The second important element came from having to solve the second problem: the union of the two large living spaces, the dining room and office, with the aim of having a large area intended for celebrations with large numbers of people. A revolving bookcase, with an eccentric shaft, was designed that, together with a sliding door that disappears inside a wall, allows these two spaces stay separate or be linked them completely.

An important unifying element of the house is the bedroom and bathroom with sloping ceilings on the second floor. Just as on the ground floor, the bathroom and bedroom are not intended to be completely closed. Instead, they consist of arranged elements that control the visual, causing the space to flow smoothly.

Location | Madrid, Spain **Area** | 3552 square feet (330 square meters) **Completion** I 2015
Design I OX architecture **Photography** I David Frutos

Living room

Curved latticework defining entrance hall

Above: Connected space between kitchen and living room for daily use

Right: Suspended kitchen counter

Above: Open bathroom located in mansard

Left: Dressing space open to bedroom

BOUNDARY

The owner of this residence is an elderly man with a great fortune and rich experience. Designing this home was primarily about a delicate balance and a gentle atmosphere.

Red, yellow, and blue historically were the colors that were associated with royalty. Yet, instead of using red or yellow, the designers deliberately set the spatial tone with blue, as its quiet elegance and deep sensibility perfectly convey the owner's state of mind. Widely used gray-level materials, such as exposed cement, gray-black veneer, together with colors of low-brightness and low chroma, are seen in the structural space, showing elegant imperfections and irregular order. At the same time, these simple colors show a sense of simplicity, and the simple design can reflect a different kind of luxury.

The entrance is extended to a dining area, where there is a large blue wall with uneven bumps on the lacquer surface. The partition wall is thickened symmetrically, which is not only creates a spatial division, but also a spiritual boundary, as if earthly life and enlightenment are separated by a line.

The space as a whole interprets 'Zen' and 'Wabi-Sabi' based on the principles of Confucianism, Taoism and Buddhism, while Song dynasty simplicity is integrated in the treatment of details.

Location | Taiwan, China **Area** | 2906 square feet (270 square meters) **Completion** | 2017
Design | Wei Yi International Design Associates **Photography** | Hey! Cheese

Exposed concrete walls in living room

Walls acting as boundaries between spaces

Dining area

Master bedroom

Bathroom

CHAMELEON

The project presents tomorrow's high-end technology, architecture and design within a stylish comfortable and surprising environment. The house is called Chameleon because, like the reptile, it too can change its colour at the touch of a button thanks to sophisticated LED light technology projecting different colors in all the rooms, creating a live work of art. Located in Son Vida, the island's most exclusive residential area, from its hilltop position, Chameleon commands panoramic views across the entire Bay of Palma and the city of Palma.

The project breaks with convention by featuring three independent houses: the main residence for living; the sports, spa and leisure house; and a large independent guest house. Walking through the main house, which is distributed on three floors, there is a sense that a huge amount of thought, creative design, and passion has gone into this extraordinary residence to create something really exemplary. Most importantly, the very best quality and master craftsmen have been used for Chameleon to create a superior finish throughout.

The interior of Chameleon includes a library, cinema, and wine cellar as well as a bar with a distinctive ceiling decoration that resembles floating drops of mercury. The walls of much of the main house are finished with a special stucco that required eight coats of paint. The second structure contains an exclusive spa and wellness area and an indoor swimming pool. In the separate building, you may find a complete guest apartment.

Due to the high-end LED construction, every room as well as Chameleon's surroundings can be transformed using any light or color mood imaginable. White was chosen as a dominant color throughout the villa to act as a perfect background for the home's spectacular illumination capabilities. Modern and clear structures as well as large glass surfaces complete this exceptional real estate.

Location | Mallorca, Spain **Area** | 26,909 square feet (2500 square meters) **Completion** | 2014
Design | APM **Photography** | APM

Kitchen with blue lighting

Lounge area

F HOUSE

This is a duplex apartment whose original layout has been largely changed. Many friends and visitors questioned the changes. Is a fully open kitchen suitable for Chinese cooking? Is the stair railing structurally sound? Is a television embedded in the wall really unnecessary? Will the grey color compromise the feeling of coziness?

However, the designer Fang Lei had faith in his design stating, 'there are a thousand Hamlets in a thousand people's eyes. The concept of family, for instance covers countless elements including people, design style, and personality.'. With many years of experience in design, Fang Lei prefers to focus on the nature of design and the experience in different spaces, rather than defining spaces with a specific label or mark. There are not so many 'whys'; the best definition of a home should be based on the needs and desires of its owner.

In the beginning, considering temporary visits from relatives and friends as well as the connection between the kitchen and the dining room, Fang Lei hesitated about whether more room should be spared for the bedroom. Later, he decided to make a thorough redefinition and re-structuring of spaces: most nonbearing walls were removed; the original bearing structure was used as the base for the interior design elements, and more dynamics were spread out among the different spaces.

In the hallway, a Moooi floor candlestick against the white wall gives a strong first impression. The original ceiling slabs were removed and the structure was enhanced. Privacy glass was used as a replacement. By adjusting the glass, you can see the terrace and enhance the lighting on this floor. The living room is connected to other spaces through openings. The uninhabited bedroom can be used as part of the living room for more guests. With the hidden bed laid down and the built-in sliding door closed, an independent bedroom turns up, which breaks the traditional living pattern and displays a more flexible space.

The wall in the original bedroom is removed and the space is integrated into the living room, forming a long hall with a study. The windows were moved and the piping along the second floor was embedded in the wall, thickening it.

A strong modernist style is expressed in the textured gray cement paint combined with solid staircase railing. The original wood finish of the steps balances the cold cement color, which displays a perfect integration of space and materials. The privacy glass strengthens the continuity between the first and the second floors. Through it, sunlight may come from the terrace into the hallway at the entrance of the first floor. On the top of the glass hides the extendable electronic window shade, which helps provide privacy. The mirror on top creates visually expands the space.

In the context of noisy city, a simple design without excessive ornaments can make a space lead to something impactful, regardless of overall style.

Location | Shanghai, China **Area** | 2583 square feet (240 square meters) **Completion** | 2015
Design | Fang Lei **Photography** | Peter Dixie

Above: Living room
Upper-Right: Lounge area near living room
Lower-Right: Kitchen

Bedroom

Bathroom

FLEXHOUSE

Flexhouse is a single-family house located on the banks of Lake Zurich in northern Switzerland. The building sits on a very narrow plot between the railway line and the local access road at the edge of the village where housing meets the countryside. The dynamic character of this location inspired the architect to develop a concept, which would interpret the transient yet tranquil nature of this plot and create soft transitions between the building, the plot, and the surrounding landscape.

Indoors, the design fluidity continues in the seamless transition between levels, unbroken views and beams of daylight, which streams throughout the space. The external curves form a beautiful backdrop inside that creates a flow through the building. The interiors are characterized by smooth spaces with no hard edges.

On the ground floor, the north-facing rear wall has many functions. In the living room, it provides a place for a storage and display, and it is the element the kitchen extends from, while the south-facing front wall is given over entirely to glazing. The sliding doors of the front façade can be completely opened up to have a direct exit to the terrace and to create a pleasantly open connection with the nature outside.

Rather than close off individual floors, the design incorporates a double-height open space that adds extra lightness to the design by visually connecting the ground floor with the first floor and delivers a glimpse of the bedrooms above.

In the master bedroom, the oak parquet partially continues in the bathroom, visually connecting the sleeping space with the bathroom. The mirror on the back wall reflects the lake, giving an exclusive view while enjoying a bath. Like in all other spaces, external blinds or internal curtains grant privacy when required.

The continuous flow between the inside and the outside culminates on the top floor, where three glazed façades and two stunning roof terraces offer stunning views over the lake and the hills beyond.

Location | Meilen, Switzerland **Area** | 1862 square feet (173 square meters) **Completion** | 2016
Design | Evolution Design **Photography** | Peter Wuermli

Dining area with large glass windows

Kitchen island

Master bedroom

Bathroom connected to master bedroom

GAME — THE JOY OF LIFE COMES FROM INFINITE EXTENSION

What is a home? In addition to being a safe haven, it is a place that accommodates and encompasses all different possibilities and forms of happiness. Besides meeting basic living requirements, the role a home plays can be richer and more varied. A home can be like a game, where interesting changes can be generated from its shape or function.

This project is one of many within an concrete urban jungle. Yet, through mixing different elements—boxes, various structures, and colors—and integrating them with a big round bucket penetrating the upper floor, the designer created an interesting space from this dull, generic concrete frame.

Gerrit Thomas Rietveld, the designer of Red and Blue Chair said, 'Structure is used to coordinate the construction, to fully guarantee the independence and integrity throughout the construction.' The same philosophy is adopted in the design of this space, showing the space through its forms, to convey a free-form image. The spatial functions can be changed at a whim just by moving around the boxes. The movable walls extend the space without limit, providing further flexibility. The space can transform from private to public in just a minute.

In the open space, there are two big round buckets of different diameters. They cut through the floor and go down, becoming a large art installation in the space. The special paint finish on the inner layer of the large round bucket shows the exquisite beauty of Asian culture, creating a kind of visual stimulation no matter from what direction you look at it. Together with the lighting design, the buckets also work as light fittings. The big round bucket, small round bucket, and the concave frame form an inverted triangle.

Boxes and round buckets in the space have different meanings: boxes with straight lines represent the rational thinking of western science, while the round buckets represent transcendental thinking within eastern philosophy. The blending of eastern and western elements creates a harmonious dialogue. The arrangement of furniture is not limited by space, objects, or direction. Multiple possible usages give new definition to the modern residence. Light is illumination as well as a guide. Through the guidance of light, you can see a space both simple yet full of eastern elegance. The wallpaper with classic Asian colors and textures, matched with copper wall lamps, creates a bright, elegant, and comfortable atmosphere.

The whole space feels just like a piece of music with high and low notes, a pleasant song rich in rhythm. The collision of low-key rustic materials and exquisite craft shows a slight sense of luxury within the modest design. At the same time, the rough texture of cement presents a kind of perfection within imperfection—a kind of spiritual yearning.

Location | Taipei, Taiwan, China **Area** | 1938 square feet (180 square meters) **Completion** | 2017
Design | Wei Yi International Design Associates **Photography** | JMS

Above: Open dining room

Left: Movable boxes allowing for flexible spatial functions

Bedroom

Bathroom

GRAY BOX

When it comes to the rural self-built housing, the stereotype image is a countrified house made of multi-story grids without any sense of design, where it costs a lot to decorate, and a lot of space is wasted.

Hidden in a distant costal village in Shantou, Gray Box is an expansion project to a rural self-built house. AD Architecture gives it a different definition. Minimalism and the pure colors of black, white, and gray add a unique landscape to this self-built house.

The owner is young and stylish, which inspired the design for a high-level gray minimalist residence. The whole space is based on the most low-key black, white, and gray, creating a textured space. Gray is highlighted to balance the strong contrast between black and white. Partial use of warm earthy yellow penetrates into the Gray Box.

The overall layout, a perfect fusion of the east and west design philosophy, is an interpretation of a pure modernist style. The proportion of lines is simple yet fine. The huge window frames beautiful scenery, and the bright light entering through the soft windows brings a Zen atmosphere.

Because of the reflection of natural light, space levels are divided by matte white paint and marble. Combined with careful consideration of the lighting layout, the space has a unique interaction between light and shadow. The skillful collocation of different materials, including leather, wood, tiles, and glass, enriches the space's overall style.

A black, white, and gray art painting is nested within this black, white, and gray space, infusing the ink-wash painting with a touch of lightness and chic. Together with the metal texture of the pieces, personal style is highlighted inadvertently. As a quiet space coupled with artistic air, this concise and smart space is immersive.

Minimalism is a complex design attitude that gets rid of overly complicated objects and avoids clutter, in order to pursue a more suitable living environment through subtraction.

Location | Shantou, Guangdong, China **Area** | 2691 square feet (250 square meters) **Completion** I 2017
Design I AD Architecture **Photography** I Ouyang Yun

Dining room

Master bedroom

HAUS BENZ

The house stands high on a plateau with stunning views across the city. The three available were divided into a public, representative space on the first floor and a private living area on the second and top floors. The first-floor public area is designed to enable a more informal and friendly contact with guests. The entrance area is a deep purple hallway that leads to individual rooms. The conference room is simultaneously designed to be used for hospitality. Its walls are painted dove grey using pigment-rich paints, which give them a particular depth. Above this color runs a broad band executed in a satiny metallic paint, which has also been used on the ceiling. The edges and corners of the walls curve gently, giving the room a soft and sensual charisma. A large round table stands upon a deep-pile rug. Above it hangs a globe light fixture, specially commissioned for the space and made from hand-blown, cut, crystal glass. A fully equipped catering kitchen on the ground floor caters to the hospitality needs of guests. A door in a mirrored dividing wall leads through to the study. The color palette here is continued with a fresh and intense blue. In the center of the room stands the Walter Knoll Keypiece desk, which appears to float on a base and sideboard.

The Cigar Lounge is a place for discussions in more relaxed surroundings. All the walls and shelves have been executed in a dark graphite grey, contrasting to the powerful mustard tone on the ceiling. Here again curved walls mark transition points and create niches in front of the windows. Semi-transparent net curtains at each window emphasize the intimate atmosphere of this room. Designers have teamed the Walter Knoll product ensemble of couch, tables, armchairs, and silk rug with an extravagant bronzed lamp, which recalls a tuning fork, and aboriginal art from the owners' collection.

The heart of the living area on the two upper floors is a generous, L-shaped room, which serves as a combined living and dining space. Storage space has been integrated against the walls leading to the staircase: cabinets with fronts that have been painted a matt shade of green. The two doorways are contained within deep recesses, with sliding doors disguised as walls. The door recess behind the dining table carries over into a shelf niche, while the recess opposite the couch holds a flat-screen television. Two pillars painted a striking orange set strong colour accents, while the dark-stained, maple, parquet floor gives the room a calm base. Contrasting with the subtle flooring is a three-dimensional, faceted ceiling. Beginning from the point of intersection of the inner walls, its polygonal folds encompass the entire room. Its triangular shapes are painted in different shades of grey, further emphasizing its folded nature. The shapes are reflected in polygonal, mirrored sections and incisions at the two end walls of the room. Here too the furniture derives almost exclusively from the Walter Knoll collection. We contrast design with artistic items from the furniture world. The table top of the long dining table, for example, is a unique original. A Persian textile was cast in tinted epoxy resin; pieces of cloth still hang out of the table top to each side.

Location | Stuttgart, Germany **Area** | 1938 square feet (180 square meters) **Completion** | 2016
Design | Ippolito Fleitz Group - Identity Architects **Photography** | Zooey Braun, Stuttgart, Germany

Above: Conference room with curved walls to hide radiators

Left: Living room

HAUS K

The Haus K project involved replanning a building that the client bought as a shell structure. Its extraordinary location in Schlossberg within Krems makes this project a crowning jewel, with a view across the valley to the river Danube, the abbey of Göttweig to the south, and the vineyards of Krems to the north.

The client's personal requirements made extensive replanning of the building's interior design necessary. The building's three levels were restructured after an analysis of the requirements. A spacious wellness area, including a sauna, whirlpool, lounge, and gym, were designed for the ground floor that leads to the northern garden.

The entrance hall is located on the floor above and connects the northern main entrance with the southern entrance to a bridge across the moat. This southern entrance can only be reached via a walkway across the Schlossberg. The bedroom with its adjacent walk-in closet, master bathroom, and a completely self-sufficient guest apartment with a garden terrace to the south are also located on this floor.

On the upper floor, a central, open staircase adjacent to the chimney wall divides the living area in a dining and living space. The open kitchen is optically separated from the living area by a wine storage refrigerator that is positioned at the staircase.

The color and material concept combines typical regional elements with an international style. The natural stone tiles, which are more often just used for terraces, were also added to the interior of the entrance area, leading up to and including the bathroom and the bedroom. Custom furniture with dark, oiled wooden fronts complete this concept.

The upper floor's materiality is characterized by gradually refined structures. Cast terrazzo flooring was used, as well as dark glass and a chimney wall made of big granite slabs, which complement the dark wooden fronts.

Location | Krems, Austria **Area** | 5920 square feet (550 square meters) **Completion** | 2017
Design | destilat **Photography** | destilat

Living room and dining room

Above: Sauna with whirlpool

Right: Master bedroom with bathroom

HOUSE 19

A-cero, managed by Joaquín Torres, presents its most minimalist project. This new house is located in a luxurious estate in Pozuelo de Alarcón in Madrid. It is one of the hundred housings that you can find already built in this exclusive housing development: an area with wide green spaces, lakes, and spectacular houses, which all have been designed by A-cero.

The structure of this new house is made of clear volumes, straight lines, and simple shapes. The house's front is made of marble travertine and there are many windows in it. Both elements give a lot of lightness to the house.

It has a surface area of 17,222 square feet (1600 square meters) and three floors. The structure adapts itself to the slope where the house is. The garage and service spaces are in the basement, while the most public spaces (lounge, dining room, living room) are on the first floor.

Bedrooms and more private rooms are on the top floor. A-cero also designed a 861-square-foot (80-square-meter) geometric swimming pool. It harmonizes with the clean architecture of this A-cero project.

Inside, the spaces are wide and full of light in every room of the house. A-cero chooses a cream polished marble for the living room and the bedrooms. The main colors inside the building are black, white, brown, and beige. The brown sofa located in the lobby on the first floor looks simple yet noble, existing in harmony with the black coffee table. Through the glass wall, you can see the pool outside. Designers highlighted the kitchen with an A-cero design that follows the thread of the project. The stove tables in the open kitchen are white. The furniture in the house combines the A-cero-designed pieces with other elements chosen by the property, focusing on simplicity and elegance as the general trend.

Location | Madrid, Spain **Area** | 17,222 square feet (1600 square meters) **Completion** | 2012
Design | A-Cero **Photography** | Luis Hernandez Segovia

Above: Interior and exterior connected through glass wall
Left: Living room

Kitchen

Lounge area

Main bedroom

Bathroom

HOUSE AN DER ACHALM

A special characteristic of the House an der Achalm is that all the rooms used for daily life are located on the top level. The projecting eastern wing facing the valley accommodates the private areas, such as bedrooms, walk-in closets, a dressing room, and bathroom.

All secondary functions are accommodated on the entrance level. The rooms for guests are located on the eastern side, while residents and guests reach the spa area by walking west past the secondary rooms and the office. A semi-roofed loggia is located in front of the spa, which directly adjoins the sun terrace and the pool.

The hall with a void and a staircase connects this part of the building with the kitchen and dining area in the western section. The corner of the adjoining living room opens up towards the terrace, which forms an introverted, enclosed space on the northern side.

A very important task was to create a certain tranquility—a visual calmness. Technical functions took a backseat as the spatial function and the role of the surfaces was more important to us in creating the overall effect. This applies for the outside as well as to the interiors.

In here, people can see the wall cladding where we tried to hide all everyday uses, such as the elevator. This creates that certain tranquility, and so a guest entering the house is not immediately bothered with everything. Common facilities like a cell phone charging station or a door opener are integrated in these panels, creating visual calmness. When sitting comfortably in front of a fireplace in the evening, a TV set would be a visual disturbance, which is why the TV set is hidden inside the wall, much like numerous other things in the house. The designers were not looking for short-lived, fashionable effects, but strived for contemporary modernity and timeless elegance.

Location | Reutlingen, Germany **Area** | 8611 square feet (800 square meters) **Completion** | 2016
Design | Alexander Brenner Architects **Photography** | Zooey Braun

Living room facing sunny side of site for great views

Kitchen and dining area

Spiral staircase

HOUSE M

House M is a residential building near Merano and is embedded in a quiet area of Obermais. The idea behind the design concept was to play with transparent and solid surfaces. This synergy creates fascinating outlooks and insights. The aim was also to melt the outside space with the interior. The terrain is meant to flow through the new building towards the pool and meadow area. Also, due to the external design and the arrangement with the pool, the green space and the placement of the building, the whole area feels in unity.

The described flow not only continues its way in the interior of the House M but it also highlights the arrangement of the building and the lawn. All these factors have been developed to create a completely natural look. The architects had the basic thought of an intelligent architecture and a daring design, which reacts to the environment, taking advantage of its characteristics. This design idea runs through the whole project.

The design and the space of the house is not at all cluttered. Also, the placement of the books on the shelves is not imprudent—some with the front facing the living room, others are stacked by size. The very minimalist kitchen is nearby the dining area. The kitchen is mostly pristine-white with a dark grey counter top.

The alternate use of black and white pairings throughout the whole building gives the house an elegant touch and personality, giving the whole a refined finishing touch. The black entry door provides a dramatic flair for the new building. A few columns and the window frames are also black, but most of the interior is white, . The master bathroom also includes a dark back splash, which is obviously a contrast to the white cabinetry and the orchids. Also, the garage has a picture of the black and white skyline of New York City. This is logically a perfect alignment to the color palette of the House M.

The wine cellar has clear geometric shapes and a granite island in the middle of the room. This storage area creates a distinctive and unmistakable ambience. The region around Bolzano is known for its good wines. This was also the reason why the villa has a wine enclave. In conclusion, this house is a perfect example of synergy between construction, art, and nature through the use of environmental ideas and artistic design themes.

Location | Merano, Italy **Area** | 3875 square feet (360 square meters) **Completion** | 2012
Design | monovolume architecture+design **Photography** | Meraner Hauser

Above: Living room
Right: Kitchen

Above: Kitchen
Right: Stairs

Master bedroom

Master bathroom

IMMERSED IN BOOKS AND GREEN

Stepping into the living room, people will get a subtle experience of comfort, created by not simply just the shade by the window, the open space, or the overall color pallette. Designer Tan Shujing cleverly combined rational and emotional thoughts into the design to balance functions and senses. Different families have different feelings and thus have different pyschological needs. The house owner has expressed his desire to create a space for family gatherings in the new house.

Cooking, dining, and reading were the top three activities for this family of four, so a dining and reading area was placed in the middle of the plan. No matter where they are in the house, this area is in the center. For the house owner, returning home to get together with his family and spending time on favorite things, such as reading, listening to music, and dining, are undoubtedly a great enjoyment in his life.

Another design focus of this project was making sure the family members could see and interact with one another even if they are in different spaces of the house, creating separate but unobstructed space.

Blue-green shade comes into view from the French windows in the living and reading area. The spatial planning has brought the greenery outside into the interior space, putting emphasis on 'unobstructed' space. Moreover, the choice of lamp in the reading area was very meticulous. On one hand, the illumination of the reading area focuses on functionality. Yet, on the other hand, the house owner's sight shall not be obstructed when he sits in the dining area and looks out the window. If a showy lamp had been installed in the reading area, it would become a distraction.

The house owner is often busy with work, while his wife does the housework. They have two daughters, one of whom is learning to paint, and the house owner loves his daughter's paintings very much. 'People are rational and strong, but sometimes are also emotional and soft.' commented Tan Shuijing. 'We have tried to arouse the emotional and soft side of the house owner by adding soft colors to the furnishings. For example, the living room sofa uses several tones of blue.'

Apart from colors, the design team wanted to make other designs in a sublter way. To make the house owner's family more relaxed when they came home, soft furniture was selected since a home is not a office. The furniture should be orderly in function and can provide sensory experiences for users. As a result, rather a large standard tea table, four small tea tables have been placed in the living room to make it easy for the house owner to arrange according to his needs.

Another challenge was to provide the required functions for each space while also instilling a sense of calmness and unity. The desk in the reading area uses the same design as the island in the middle of the dining area, making the middle island and the desk form a smooth line when looked at from the dining area.The visual effect draw people's attention to the landscape out of window, giving a 'distinct but not scattered' unity in space. Chandeliers over the table are made of bright stainless steel, accenting the character of the dining area.

Location | Taiwan, China **Area** | 1830 square feet (170 square meters) **Completion** | 2016
Design | Herzu Design **Photography** | moooten studio

Living room

Reading area

Bedroom

Bathroom

LIGHT OF LIFE

The design team needed to transcend the restriction of framework and style, instill a calming atmosphere, and heighten spatial awareness The client aquired an empty house that he hoped to enlarge through design. Empty is not devoid of substance, but revealed in visual perception and modernist approach. The designer used 'Less is more' approach to take away the common definition of space, removing unnecessary decorationand giving the field the largest scale and flexibility.

In this case, the design team focused on the lighting design in the hallway of the public space. The oblique lines extend to the façade. They customized points illumination and placed them in triangle boxes, creating uniform illumination throughout the space. There is a small groove on the left side of the entrance as a way of guiding and creating atmosphere.

The living and dinning area uses ring-like lines, getting rid of dated arrangements of furniture and adapting a humanist perspective in design. The basic tone of the space makes it function both as a background and extension. The designer uses different materials yet with similar color sense, such as slices of glossy tiles and light gray finishing, to make acohesive visual experience, from the luster of stainless steel to the outline of the lamps.

The use of light gray paint on the large cabinet door ensures a smooth visual transition. The parallel sliding door is easy to use, and together with the cabinet, it will blend in effortlessly in the space when closed, given the two doors are of the same thickness. The concept of 'Light of Life' runs through the spatial design. Light plays an important role in the visual effect as well as arranging the space, connecting the metal ceiling above the public and private area with the hand-sprayed acrylic lamps.

The kitchen was designed from the perspective of the users, taking cooking needs into account, such as storage position and lighting requirements, yet it continues to use the same materials as the overall space uses. The door of balcony with large louvers achieves visual conformity, using light that penetrates from window gaps to create a pleasant atmosphere.

The guest bathroom is small, so white ceramic tiles with embossing were used to increase the sense of space. The master bathroom can gain abundant natural light due to its double-faced lighting French windows; The stainless steel frame combines storage and piping together, showing delicate textures against imitation stone tiles. The children's bathroom continues in the same style as the bedroom.

The master bedroom uses Thai silk cover the wall, whose fine texture has a bit of light gray luster, presenting a tranquil space for people. The embedded stainless steel wall lamps have been used to embellish contours and establish a living context.

Location | Taiwan, China **Area** | 3014 square feet (280 square meters) **Completion** | 2016
Design | Herzu Design **Photography** | Wu Qimin

Above: Living room
Right: Kitchen

Walk-in closet

Main bedroom

Bathroom

MC3 HOUSE

The MC3 House is part of a residential development scheme of three dwellings located in a garden city in the outskirts of Barcelona. The importance of vegetation in this urban context gave place to taking the living space into account very closely right from the beginning of the design process. The dwelling defines the garden and vice versa.

The layout of the house is in a L-shape floor plan on only one level, in order to give all of the rooms views onto the swimming pool and garden. The intention of the interior design was to achieve minimal, warm spaces with just a few materials, such as white plaster on the walls, the grey tiles for the flooring, and the walnut wood for doors and furniture. The wooden panels are made of vertical strips, which are also used to make the large sliding doors that allow connection to other spaces, such as the living room and the kitchen. The micro-cement walls in the bathrooms, smooth and without texture, allow incorporating decoration and lighting elements that allow the centrer of attention to be focused on other elements, such as a lamp or a painting.

The flat roof is separated on two different levels, the lower one for use at night and the higher one acting as a living room, enhancing the indoor-outdoor relationship in the day area. Two inner courtyards with plants and sweetgum trees confirm the role of nature in the dwelling's design. The first courtyard separates the day wing from the night and allows one to see the outside from the entrance hall. The second one provides natural light to the bathrooms and also disrupts the narrowness of the corridor.

Location | Barcelona, Spain **Area** | 3552 square feet (330 square meters) **Completion** | 2016
Design | Mogas Arquitectes and Anna Vallmitjana **Photography** | José Hevia

Living room and dining room

Stairs to upper floor

Open kitchen

Bedrooms

Sinks

Bathroom

Shower

MONOLITHIC HOUSE

The Monolithic House is an apartment located in Castrovillari in southern Italy that got its name from the creative concept behind the project: explorations with the volumetric subtractions of a monolithic block. The majestic views of the Pollino massif mountains, clearly visible from the luminous windows of the apartment, led to the choice of stone as the conceptual raw material. In addition to stone, the other predominant natural material is wood, which warms the environment from the entrance, a place immediately enveloped in a surreal atmosphere with a rain of Swarovski crystals adorning the walls.

The project is a clear example of minimalist inspiration. In fact, reducing to the bare essence is a concept used not only in the functional division of the spaces that revolve around the open plan but also in the use of integrated elements in the environment of the architecture. The main active element of the interior design around is the monolithic block, the stone wall's partition between kitchen and living room, characterized by a window performing the dual function of table and support plane. The bathrooms are the triumph of total white, one featuring damask textures, the other one with curved reliefs.

The careful use of lighting enhances the rigor of spaces, intensifying the volumes especially at the entrance, where a floating ceiling, pierced by a bright cut, introduces dynamism to the other environments. The choice of minimalist design elements as the total white—the wallpaper with contemporary lettering, the handmade furniture, and the ethereal glass walls—creates a visual balance, a hierarchical order forming visual weight that is easy to read.

Location | Castrovillari, Italy **Area** | 1830 square feet (170 square meters) **Completion** | 2014
Design | Brain Factory - Architecture & Design **Photography** | Marco Marotto

View of monolithic block

Window in kitchen

Above: Bathroom
Left: Hallway near living room

MUSICIAN'S RESIDENCE IN NAOUSA

This summer house is situated in Naoussa, at the island of Paros in the Cyclades islands. It is a quiet neighborhood in the eastern part of the town, very close to the beautiful sandy beach of Saint Anargyros.

The project is a house for a family of musicians. The house's white volumes are structural and remain simple and cubic. They follow the voids and masses of the neighboring buildings, expanding from the scenary to the sea, becoming part of its context. The thick inclined walls are inspired from the island's monastic architecture. The walls revolve around the swimming pool and the interior 'protected' courtyard, a microcosm of the house.

Exterior space flows in a spiral way from the ground floor courtyard to the terrace on the top with a magnificent view to the sea and the town of Naoussa. Next to the pool is the music studio, which serves also as a guest room.

Materials used are simple and minimalist: concrete floors and roofs and dark grey frames contrast with the white Cycladic walls. Concrete stucco on the bathroom walls and fireplace contrasts with modern forms, like the black granite kitchen. A minimalist and ascetic language is expressed in a modern contemporary way, a language with many affinities to Greek culture.

The house follows the principles of bioclimatic design. Good thermal insulation on the roofs and an exterior rapping of the walls provided by a new technology thermal insulation system protect the interior space from extreme weather conditions created by northern winds on this part of the island.

The house works in a multifaceted manner, with its main façade on the street becoming a movie screen during the night, where the wind creates a mute choreography of the shadows of the plants projected.

Location | Cyclades, Greece **Area** | 1938 square feet (180 square meters) **Completion** | 2016
Design | GEM Architects **Photography** | Costas Vergas

View of living room and kitchen area

View of music studio

Master bedroom

Bathroom

OVER WHITE

The costumers wanted to give a new life for their house, which was 14 years old. They needed a new modern house, which would be appropriate for their lifestyle. The family consists of two adults and two children. The location near the river gave us an idea to integrate the beautiful nature of this area into the interior and use more natural light to enlarge the space.

The living room and the bedroom are decorated with contrasting black and white, and the entire space has few furniture or decorations, showing a minimalist living space. By the main entrance is an attached dressing room and a new entrance. The old entrance was turned into a music room, which connected the kitchen and living room. The idea 'without borders' was developed with the stairs and in the lobby of the second floor. There are no railings.

Designers rebuilt four narrow windows in the living room into one panoramic, adding an expressive façade and modernizing it, making the interior an integral part of the landscape. Also, there is a wooden window sill, which is a perfect place to sit with a book or newspaper. The kitchen is functional and minimalistic. The house is equipped with air recovery system and air conditioning, and the lights can be operated by iPhone or iPad.

Location | Krivoy Rog, Ukraine **Area** | 2722 square feet (211 square meters)   **Completion** | 2014
Design | Azovskiy + Pahomova Architects   **Photography** | T. Kovalenko

Monochrome interior

Living space with Porcelanosa tile

PENTHOUSE AMSTERDAM

The large surface of this penthouse on the third floor of a canal house in the center of Amsterdam requested an open attitude.Thanks to some bold architectural interventions, the potential of different spaces were uncovered. The 30-foot (9-meter) kitchen and the large fireplace in the living area catch the eye, as well as the kitchen island with integrated dining table. With their large dimensions, they bring balance and peace to the interior The sofa, table, and grey carpet are comfortable but luxurious. The bathroom and storage space are located behind a façade. The darker shade contrasts with the light floor. Thereby, the effect of the interventions is emphasized. In the bedroom, the main colors used are white and brown. There are no extra decorations in the bedroom, presenting a sense of simplicity.

From furniture and accessories to layout and architecture, the starting point for Remy Meijers in all his interior design was finding perfectly matching elements. That is why he almost always chooses furniture and accessories that he designs himself. Some of these items can be found in this project as well.

Location | Amsterdam, The Netherlands **Area** | 2422 square feet (225 square meters) **Completion** | 2015
Design | Remy Meijers **Photography** | René Gonkel

Dining and living area

Bathroom counter

PENTHOUSE GRIFFINTOWN

Penthouse Griffintown is located in a new residential complex juxtaposed to the Lachine Canal. The 2722-square-foot (211-square-meter) residence offers sublime perspectives on Montreal's natural and urban landscapes.

The concept focuses on the environment by bringing views and natural light into the home. Upon entry, a central corridor directs the eye outward and organizes the house in two parts. To the west, a branch leads to the master suite and a children's room with bathroom. To the east, there is an office, an entertainment room and a guest room which also serves as a play room. The living areas are located to the south in a large open area that allows the homeowners to admire sunrises and sunsets, while also providing space for the family to share moments together.

The kitchen, all in black, contrasts with the white oak floors that soften the hardness of exposed concrete. The precise organization of the rooms and the delicacy of the interior design have made it possible to create a bold and luminous sanctuary in relation with the beauty of the site.

The kitchen, pantry, and wine cellar were designed as one visual block, unifying consistent materials to create a sense of drama. Meticulously planned to maximize functional needs, towers for storage wrap around the kitchen, concealed by full-height doors that appear as wall panels.

An abundance of natural light inspired a dark palette of charcoals and a tone-on-tone approach. To maintain an understated expression, matte finishes were favoured.

Oak floors, an important organic element to the space, add warmth, softening the bold cabinetry and their imposing proportions. The decision to leave the concrete ceilings and columns exposed was influenced by the industrial architectural details inherent to the neighbourhood. A custom brass suspension provides contrast and serves as a sculptural counterpoint to the minimalistic design of the room.

Location | Montreal, Canada **Area** | 2722 square feet (253 square meters) **Completion** | 2016
Design | MXMA Architecture & Design with Catlin Stothers Design **Photography** | Drew Hadley

Living and dining room areas connected

Media rooms

Main bedroom and bathroom

PURIFIED RESIDENCE

People often have a special bond to certain memories. Channeling these past life experiences as well as creating new ones for the client was the core for this project.

In this project, white is the most element for memory. This simple element is used throughout the space using many different blocks, shaping the functional spaces of every floor and creating a clear, cozym and refined atmosphere. The flake-shaped stairs and glittery chandeliers penetrate and connect all floors, making all functional spaces both divided and connected. In this way, the space gets rid of rigorous geometrical shapes and creates a relaxed atmosphere.

For the first floor, a 'box' positioned in the center divides the whole space into living room, dining area (including open kitchen), sub-living room, and reading room. The box placed in the center is the core of the space. The floating stairs with two steps raised sharpen the boundaries between areas within the space. The large-scale window ensures good ventilation and plenty of light in the space and, at the same time, corresponds with the courtyard outside, allowing the residents to easily experience the changing seasons.

Space required by children growing up is the main connecting link to the second floor. Designers added some bright colors and irregular shapes in this soft and warm space, creating a warm environment that fits the active nature of children. The third floor is the master bedroom. The main bathroom in the middle is like a hidden box that divides the master bedroom into sleeping area and changing area.

The basement is the reception area. Artworks are used to make divisions and transform tonality in the staircase. Grey and black are taken as main colors on this floor, making this space magnificent with a certain sense of Zen.

The whole design is restrained, fulfilling the needs of the entire family.

Location | Nanjing, China **Area** | 7965 square feet (740 square meters) **Completion** | 2016
Design | Wei Yi International Design Associates **Photography** | JMS

The Way of Love

Love is patient and kind; love does not
envy or boast; it is not arrogant or rude.
It does not insist on its own way; it is not
irritable or resentful; it does not rejoice
at wrongdoing, but rejoices with the truth.
Love bears all things, believes all things,
hopes all things, endures all things. Love
never ends.

Kitchen

Stairwell

Children's play area

Children's room

Above: Main bedroom

Bottom and right: Bathroom in main bedroom

Above: Basement wine tasting area
Upper-Left: Basement living room
Lower-Left: Basement entrance

RÉSIDENCE DE L'AVENUE LAVAL

The project is located in one of most attractive and central neighbourhoods in Montreal, the 'Plateau Mont-Royal.' As it is very dense, finding a virgin plot to construct a new house seemed like an impossible task. As a result, the designers' strategy was to transform a duplex into a single-family cottage to provide the minimalist oasis of calm coveted by the client and his family. The existing building is typical of Montreale's typology. It is organized by length, and the rooms are delivered by a long corridor. The lack of windows, as it is just possible to create openings on the front and rear façades, generates a very dark and unwelcoming atmosphere. Consequently, several architectural strategies were elaborated to convert this old duplex into a contemporary, pleasant, and luminous house.

A central void was created to invite the sun and natural light to bathe the living spaces. This opening emphasizes the impressive double-height open staircasethat takes place as the spinal column of the project. Sizable windows, light shafts, and glass panels generate transparency as well as an airy and spacious living area. The ceiling seems to disappear. The central void unifies the space by removing the partitions between them and lets the light spread around the house.

On the ground floor, the space is divided by the screen of a storage unit that structures the entrance of the rest of the space. The living spaces, such as the kitchen and the living room with its impressive fireplace, are organized into a large open area, structured by the central opening. Upstairs, the master bedroom and two other rooms are distributed on both sides of the central void. Some glass panels increase the light coming in from the glass ceiling.

Location | Montréal, Canada **Area** | 1850 square feet (172 square meters) **Completion** | 2016
Design | ADHOC Architectes **Photography** | Jean-François St-Onge

Above: Open area on first floor
Upper-Right: Staircase
Lower-Right: Master bedroom

RESIDENCE OAK

This small residence was built in a quiet place. The clear, simple wooden volumes were applied to highlight the wooded context that surrounds it. Despite its distinctive contemporary appearence, the residence fits the site perfectly, far from the frenzy of the city.

The project consisted in the renovation of a house in Québec City, Canada. The owners wished to adapt their residence to their new lifestyle, and the living space needed a face-lift. For this residence, the interior spaces have been reconfigured to maximize natural light. Vertical windows were added, and the dining room opens to the outside for the family to overlook the backyard and the natural scenery. The kitchen, which is the core of the design, also takes advantage of big openings and distinguishes itself by a wide island and a very minimalist style. The integrated furniture hides a washbasin and cupboard, which are all-white. As for the lighting, which was also very important for the drawing room, simple color and style was chosen to maintain the minimalist concept, while some details reveal the luxurious texture. The one-piece design of the dining table and washbasin, with a simple and upscale look, can not only save space, but also provide an increased functional expression.

A simple wooden staircase leads upstairs. The wooden floor is harmonious with the overall white space, combining a wide walk-in and a shower room. There, the white wooden washstand also shows a minimal tone. This room also takes advantage of the back of the house and establish a quiet place for looking at the woods. This set of simple volumes created a simple residence that was still remaining minimalist and elegant.

Location | Québec City, Canada **Area** | 5345 square feet (500 square meters) **Completion** | 2017
Design | Hatem+D **Photography** | Dave Tremblay, Charles O'hara

Above: Living room with view of garden
Right: Open kitchen connecting to dining area

Above: Bathroom with view outside

Left: View of kitchen and stairs

ROCA LLISA

As annual visitors to the island of Ibiza, the owners stipulated a contemporary reinvention of the classic Mediterranean villa they had purchased at the top of a wooded hill in the exclusive Roca Llisa area. The design had to mediate between the functions of a family retreat, a meditative space, and a fully functioning entertainment venue.

The interior design and décor needed to be simultaneously casual and elegant. The main style of this house is modern minimalism, and color white is widely used in the decoration, which highlights the warm and simple atmosphere. The design approach was to focus on the use of natural organic materials, such as timber and stone. Textured materials add warmth and depth to the minimal and clean interior. Large sliding, glass doors allow the natural surroundings to form part of the interior. Each space on the three levels provides for different functions and exhibits its own particular nuances.

OKHA was the main furniture supplier and provided South African pieces custom-made for the clients. ARRCC used a soft, naturally inspired color palette where the use of varying materials and textures added depth and resonated an effortless, organic sense of luxury. Cottons, linens, raw timber, stone, and marble against a backdrop of fresh white walls give the internal spaces a natural calm and serenity; the eclectic mix of contemporary designs, artisanal pieces and one-off custom creations reflect the clients' broad appreciation and understanding of art and design as well as their desire for luxury contemporary living where every moment counts and a home provides the literal foundations of a balanced lifestyle.

Location | Ibiza, Spain **Area** | 9096 square feet (845 square meters) **Completion** | 2015
Design | ARRCC **Photography** | Lorenzo Vecchia

Accents of color add interest to the neutral palette of the pool lounge, the large glass doors stack away and allow the natural surroundings to form part of the interior

Clean, horizontal and vertical lines are emphasized in this minimalist kitchen design, a live edge walnut timber counter top adds a warm layer to the space

Above and left: The formal seating area features a custom-made solid French oak coffee table with brass inserts and leather straps

Ample natural light gives the master bedroom and en-suite a serene feeling. The bed is raised on a timber platform which wraps up behind the bed. A concealed door in the wall panel creates an uninterrupted backdrop

SOL HOUSE

The site is situated along a residential road with buildings primarily dating from the 1930s, typical for Stuttgart's hillside locations. The residence relates to the down-to-earth quality and the scale of the neighboring two-story, cubic houses, but the façade facing the street is, owed to modern living requirements, mainly closed.

The cubism of the external forms impacts on the interior, applying to the everyday utility objects in the living rooms, kitchen and bathroom. Not only are all the cupboards in this house adapted to the order of the spatial continuum's subtle rhythms, but so are all the objects within the space.

The ground floor accommodates the jointly used rooms, such as the kitchen and the dining and living area. The upper level is reserved for guests and, most of all, the parents. Making use of a cross slope, both the ground floor and the garden level below have a ground-level access to the southeast garden. The garden level provides plenty of space for the children as well as space for a sauna with a relaxation room. The living areas open up in a downhill direction towards the forest in the south. All furniture and fittings were understood as an integral part of the overall architecture and were thus planned by the architect from the beginning.

In the center of the house, built-in units are primarily used for storage but also hide elements like the lift door and access to the garden level. Additionally, they is the interface between people and technology. These units also accommodate structural components and technical installations, but their appearance has completely freed itself from such digital complexities. Consequently, they can function as a calm screen in front of which the inhabitants' lives play out.

Great diligence and simplicity was again the wish and aim for the design of the dining area. Except for the ceiling luminaries by Verner Panton, only the connection to the outside and a picture of nature act as decorative elements. The cantilevered chairs by Thonet are, like all other seating furniture, proven design classics. When reducing to the essential, to bare functions, simplicity and beauty is the result.

Location | Stuttgart, Germany **Area** | 4661 square feet (433 square meters) **Completion** | 2014
Design I Alexander Brenner Architects **Photography** I Zooey Braun

Above: Living area

Right: Open hallway with view of outdorrs

Above: Staircase to second floor

Right: Dining area

SU HOUSE

On a plot in a villa quarter, at the edge of a forest in the south of Stuttgart, a villa in minimalist style thoroughly designed down to the smallest detail was built for an art lover and her family.

From the piazza at the entrance to the site, a silvery garage structure leads past the upper garden with the lake and the 'morning patio' with its pebble stone flooring to the entrance on the north side. Beyond the entrance hall, the large dining table is placed below a two-story void and is lit by a skylight.

The movable floor-to-ceiling glazing opens up at a right-angle to the terrace, so that the inside merges with the covered outside in the summer months. The kitchen was designed as an eat-in kitchen. It works either as a closed space, or, thanks to the wide sliding door, as a part of the whole.

A large, broad fireplace directs to the living area, which was planned as a more secure and intimate place. A full-width skylight at the back sends light onto the wall with paintings and sculptures. From the southern study and workspace, a narrow sculptural staircase leads down to the studio. This two-story-high, almost sacral area serves to present works of art—a passion of the client. Right next to the studio, a storeroom for artwork is attached. The majority of the garden level consists of the pool and spa area.

The sauna and steam bath are in an introverted area kept entirely in warm red and gold tones. The indoor swimming pool, on the other hand, opens with a floor-to-ceiling glazing towards the lower south-west part of the garden.

In the upper storey all bedrooms and the corresponding bathrooms are arranged around the gallery. The master bedroom with fireplace, dressing room, and bathroom is designed as an interconnected 'private area.' The covered roof terrace, positioned in front of the bedroom, offers a mile-wide view to southwest. Even more breathtaking is the view from the overlying roof terrace.

Location | Stuttgart, Germany **Area** | 3552 square feet (330 square meters) **Completion** | 2012
Design | Alexander Brenner Architects **Photography** | Zooey Braun

Living room with rustic feel

Kitchen

Above: Custom-design tables designed to be connected together

Right: Outdoor terrace

Master bedroom with built-in projector system

Swimming with views of adjacent garden

SUITE FOR TEN

This Barcelona flat can accommodate up to ten without requiring a single sleeping bag. The other ten can eat at the same time, and if people are just chatting, then another ten can easily fit into the space. The flat's broad social area is organized into three contiguous living areas annexed to a large open kitchen well, allowing density while promoting interactions. Meanwhile, in its more private half are three en-suite bedrooms, each with their own walk-in closet bathroom. An entrance hall is a 'green' oasis in the very heart of this family suite, reconciling seeming opposites: elegance and practicality, neutrality and distinctiveness, indoors and outdoors, and metallic sheen with the freshness of vegetation. All these contrasts are combined under a single interior scheme that aims to bring light where there is little and, above all, to provide comfort.

Comfort and simplicity are key in this suite. However, what perhaps is most distinctive about this space is its actual storage capacity: generous dressing rooms flanked by cabinets made with textile laminates, glass partitions, and polished mirrors over wooden vanity tops.

Here, the furniture repertoire expands itself to accommodate the most diverse forms of recreation, combining benches, stools, ottomans, sofas, and armchairs with side tables, desks and libraries, all under an adjustable and sensual lighting scheme. The result is an experience that manages to transition between day and night, ort from breakfast to party time, as easy and natural as possible. When you stay in the space, you can feel the energy coming from such simple atmosphere.

Location | Barcelona, Spain **Area** | 1851 square feet (172 square meters) **Completion** | 2016
Design | Egue y Seta **Photography** | VICUGO FOTO

Above: Living room

Right: Kitchen with plants

Panorama of kitchen and dining area

Cooking area

Bedroom

Bathroom

S.V. HOUSE

A-cero presents a new single-family house located in the southern Spain designed with orthogonal shapes but following a strict criteria. It is a luxury home in a residential area on the outskirts of the city of Seville. This house is characterized by its facing with travertine marble and black glass. They wanted a high-class visual appearance made with durable materials.

The distribution of the house starts from the street, where people enter directly into the basement to the of garage and warehouse. From there, people can find an elevator that connects all three levels. The ground floor, which is also the main floor, houses the most of the public and living areas of the house, except for a wing on this floor reserved for the large master bedroom with its two bathrooms and two seperate dressing rooms. The rest of the house consists of two living rooms, a dining room, a cinema room, a kitchen, and an office. From the entrance hall to the ground floor stands out a lamp designed in golden metal and mahogany wood. Below, a circular table in lacquered black wood is accompanied on a wall with white lined paneling and a sideboard in black lacquer. On this floor, as on the upper floor, the façade stone is polished as a floor finish.

In the dining room, there is a table with a black glass envelope surrounded by Klee chairs from A-cero upholstered in gray velvet from Lizzo. The whole space can hold up to 16 people. The steel ceiling lamp is a key feature in the room. A large sliding door can separate the dining room from the living room.

The great hall takes advantage of high ceilings that receives direct light from the deck, creating a universe of natural light. The space is furnished with two large gray sofas made by L of Minotti and two caramel armchairs by Barcelona of Mies de Knollr. The main wall is presided over by a painting by Joaquin Torres and Rafael Llamazares, and the furnishings of the room are complemented by a coffee table.

Located separately on the same floor is the master bedroom. A large partition separates the dressing area and the two separate bathrooms. The floor is made of marble, and, in the bathrooms and showers, it also becomes vertical. The faucet is Gessi and Porcelanosa ceramics. Also, in these rooms, the presence of light was carefully considered. In the large bedroom, there is a bed with headboard covered in cowhide skin from Graces Gracia, two bedside aubergine gray tables in lacquered wood with a metallic circular handle design from Minotti's Archipenko line. The bedroom is complemented with a desk, a bedside table, a cozy reading room with white leather armchairs, a circular center table with a glass envelope, and a gray pearl silk rug from India.

Location | Sevilla, Spain **Area** | 3229 square feet (300 square meters) **Completion** | 2016
Design | A-Cero **Photography** | Victor Sajara

Dining room

Kitchen

Lounge area connected to outdoor pool

Sofa in living room

Bedroom

Study room on first floor

Bedroom

Bathroom

THE BLACK CORE HOUSE

Axelrod Architects transformed a single-family house in Tel Aviv to reflect the homeowners' love of serenity and sleek modern design as well as the firm's vision of modern residential architecture. The new homeowners wanted to remodel an existing 1980's house to reflect their indoor-outdoor lifestyle. Their family life is now centered around a lush landscaped courtyard just outside their living-dining space. Axelrod Architects organized the house around a new 'Black Core,' a glossy, black glass elevator that connects the living spaces below to the private sleeping spaces above. The Black Core House espouses the Axelrod's modern visual language, influenced by numerous International Style and Bauhaus buildings found in modern Tel Aviv.

The glass surface of the black core inside reflects images of landscape throughout the house, reinforcing the idea of living in nature. The simple clarity of contrasting surfaces, whether black and white or glossy and matte, is one of the unifying characteristics repeated in the interior design and the architecture of the building envelope. The overall tone is 'black and white.' Walls and stairs present black and white contrast. Kitchen utensils and furniture are very simple in color and design, without complex colors, showing a minimalist living space.

The living space opens out to nature with clear sliding glass openings, while expanding upward to the bedroom level with open balconies and a double-height ceiling. An open reading/media area tucked away upstairs allows the family to see each other, while still finding quiet space for relaxation.

The entry façade of white concrete and matte stucco is perforated by vertical openings and horizontal slits that reveal the indoor-outdoor nature of the home within, presenting a sleek modernist face to a quiet, upscale neighborhood of Tel Aviv.

Location | Tel Aviv, Israel **Area** | 5500 square feet (510 square meters) **Completion** | 2016
Design | Axelrod Architects **Photography** | Amit Geron

Above: Kitchen
Upper-right: Stairs to living room
Bottom-right: Reading area

THE W.I.N.D. HOUSE

The internal organization of The W.I.N.D. House is defined by its external conditions. The more intimate working and sleeping areas are located towards the back, where the enclosure of the nearby woods provides an intimate, private setting, while the open-plan living areas enjoy expansive and panoramic views of the typical Dutch polder landscape to the front. The vertical organization of the house follows a split-level principle. An open staircase at the center of the house connects the front and back wings, with the result that each turn on the stair provides expansive vistas through the house and out towards the surrounding landscape.

Furniture mainly in creamy-white give a feeling of simplicity and neatness. The open-plan living area and kitchen area are located on the first floor. Here, one front wing serves as the living space, where the back wall houses storage, an open fireplace, and a cushioned bench, all of which are integrated into one built-in furniture element. Seating in the living area includes the My Chair, designed by Ben van Berkel for Walter Knoll, and the Flexform sofa by Evergreen. The coffee table, Leolux, is by Cimber and the carpet is from Perletta Carpets.

The dining area with an open kitchen is positioned in the adjacent front wing, with both wings being separated by a recess. A wooden podium for display, which curves around this glazed recess, softly connects the living and the dining area. The kitchen table, Seven, is by B&B Italian and the Flow Chairs are by MDF Italian. The light above the dining table is the Norman-Copenhagen Bell.

From the living areas, the staircase leads up to the second level towards the rear of the house, where the master bedroom with a hamam and the guest room are located. The walls and seating element in the hamam are finished with a Moroccan tadelakt, made from limestone with a finishing of olive-oil and supplied by Tierrafino in Amsterdam. An open bath by Jean-Marie Massaud and supplied by from Axor Massaud is located next to the window in the master bedroom. The floors and walls of the three bathrooms in the house are clad with natural pebble stones, while the bathroom appliances are from the Grohe range from Axor Massaud.

Almost all of the floors in the house are homogeneously covered with a PU-coating in soft tones to increase the fluid connection between all areas. The sleeping areas have a slightly darker tone to emphasize the intimacy of these spaces. For acoustic reasons, oak flooring is employed in the music room. The natural clay stucco of the walls and ceilings strengthens the natural appearance and the connection with the landscape.

Location | Noord-Holland, the Netherlands **Area** | 4370 square feet (406 square meters) **Completion** | 2014
Design | UNStudio **Photography** | Inga Powilleit

Above: Dining area used for family activities
Left: Kitchen

Above: Sinks in master bathroom

Left: Living room outfitted with a variety of custom-designed furniture

VILLA B

Eclectic elegance, charming tranquility, and discrete luxury are the key defining features of minimalistic design, unlike the negative description often visualized: cold, stern and impersonal. In this specific residence, the designer Elena Karoula, composed the interior space with an architectural emphasis on the flow between internal and external spaces, utilizing the positive characteristics of the minimalistic design approach.

The sense of continuity in the space is emphasized by the uniform use of grey Cretan marble in a matt antique finish. It starts from the entrance steps, moves inside through the surrounding veranda, and ends at the lower level by the internal staircase. Unfolding further into the garden, the marble extends itself more via the linear steps surrounding the swimming pool, thus clinging together exterior and interior spaces. The use of grey/black mosaics for the swimming pool lining materializes a sculptural expression of 'tone on tone' as exposed to the natural or artificial illumination depending on the time of the day. This contemporary design philosophy allows the visitors to function and interact within the spaces, rather than view them as exhibition spaces to be only observed.

Moving through the spaces, one experience the positive characteristics of the minimalistic design approach blended with elaborate ornaments and details envisioned by Elena Karoula. As she explained, 'I started creating, looking forward without leaving out the references to classical forms and elements. It is a fact to me that the two styles of modern and classical have more in common than their respective supporters would concede. I am charmed by the blending of modernistic ideas as they spring from traditional classical references.'

This specific residence is made of two functional subsets, at two distinct levels and is surrounded by the rich vegetation of the exterior environment. This building is characterized by its large scale which maximizes the minimalistic approach through three-dimensional forms, natural and artificial lighting, as well as transparencies and reflections. Special attention was paid to the night time illumination, transforming the garden into 'another room,' is adding to the sequence of the interior spaces and thus maximizing the 'magic' of this residence.

Location | Ekali, Athens, Greece **Area** | 6997 square feet (650 square meters) **Completion** | 2012
Design | elena Karoula design.architecture **Photography** | Dimitris Kleanthis

Above: Open living area

Right: Kitchen overlooking exterior dining veranda

Master Suite with private veranda

Guest bathroom

VILLA LE TRIDENT ON THE CÔTE D'AZUR

The American architect of the Modernist movement, Barry Dierks, built numerous villas from 1925 to the 1950s on the French Riviera. His architecture remains a characteristic feature of the Mediterranean coast to this day, particularly since most of his buildings are heritage-protected. Still, probably one of the best-known owners of one of Barry Dierks' villas was the British novelist and playwright William Somerset Maugham. The Villa Le Trident, was built in 1926. After the Villa Le Trident was sold in 2011, 4a Architekten received the commission to completely renovate the building. The architects focused on preserving Barry Dierks' architectural legacy while giving the ageing villa a modern ambience.

The white, cubic architecture of the villa's exterior continues to captivate. The designers picked up this distinctive appearance and developed it further in a contemporary manner. Since the redesign, the prevailing impression is one of spaciousness, the suffusion of light and simple elegance. A large part of the interior walls on the first and second floors were removed, creating a fluid transition between the different areas. The living and dining area with an open-plan kitchen as well as a library are located on the ground floor. The second floor provides space for four bedrooms, each of which has its own en-suite bathroom. Long window façades offer superb views of the sea. White, suspended furniture, white curtains on the external walls, solid oak floorboards and glass elements lend a bright and tranquil atmosphere to the rooms. Distinctive features include individual elements such as the furniture, a fireplace suspended from the ceiling, and the wall element designed by the architects in the library. The teak panelled, free-standing cubes are another eye-catching feature on both floors. In order to retain the splendid views, the bathrooms, dressing room, and vertical ducts were detached from the external walls and integrated into the teak cubes. The linear lighting along their bottom edges brings out the character of the fitted furniture, creating atmospheric, illuminated highlights within the room. Sliding glass doors have been installed, allowing the sea views from the long window façades to remain uninterrupted and the flowing impression of space to continue.

Two further guest rooms are located on the ground floor. The entrance hall and stairwell were also rebuilt as part of the refurbishment. In its exposed position on a rocky outcrop, the swimming pool was reshaped and similarly modernized, while the grounds were also redesigned.

Location | Théoule-sur-Mer, France **Area** | 3552 square feet (330 square meters) **Completion** | 2014
Design | 4a Architekten GmbH **Photography** | Uwe Ditz

Living/dining area area with kitchen in background

Dining area with fireplace in background

Top: Living room
Bottom: Kitchen

Top: Teak paneled cube in center as key feature in visuals
Bottom: Bathroom inside teak panelled cube

WAVERLY RESIDENCE

Waverly Residence, located just south of Jean-Talon Street in the Alexandra-Marconi district, is the result of the idea of creating a very modern living place for wealthy clients in this up-and-coming neighborhood. The overall home decoration embodies minimalist style. The design for the lighting and furniture conveys a sense of luxury. The simple lines for the whole space brings out elegant details, creating a comfortable space.

The project started with a duplex, with almost all of the existing structure entirely rebuilt. Extra space was added on the two floors near the rear of the old building. Moreover, by excavating the basement, the residence went from 1500 square feet (139 square meters) to 3000 square feet (278 square meters). On the same lot, facing south-west, a large courtyard was added to enjoy the sun.

Once the threshold is crossed, the lobby extends across the entire width of the building. Ahead is a wall with full-height doors. These give access to a storage space dep enough for strollers and sports equipment to the left as well as a locker room to the right. On both ends, a corridor leaves a choice to go left or right to access the rest of the residence. These arrangements are part of a large volume comprising also the stairs and the kitchen towards the back of the residence. In fact, the stairs act as an incision through this volume all the way to the roof. A large skylight with same width as the stairwell allows light to flood the center of the house. Two large cubes dictate the configuration of the space. True to their philosophy, MU Architecture wanted to design an architecture that confronts, destabilizes and fascinates.

The wooden steps, inserted between the two parallel walls without silt, seem to levitate. The shadow line formed by the light above accentuates this effect. A large window closes the large opening to the kitchen, allowing it to also benefit from the presence of skylights. This same transparent wall creates a surprising illusion that the staircase landing is the extension of the kitchen counter. In the living room, the monumental fireplace covered with raw steel panels divides the space into two areas. Large sliding windows fill the back wall with an opening to the terrace in the courtyard. All the rooms on the ground floor are generously filled with unobtrusive natural light that accentuates the theatrical effect of the place.

Location | Montreal, Canada **Area** | 3000 square feet (278 square meters) **Completion** | 2015
Design | MU Architecture **Photography** | Julien Perron-Gagné

Above: Living area
Right: Kitchen

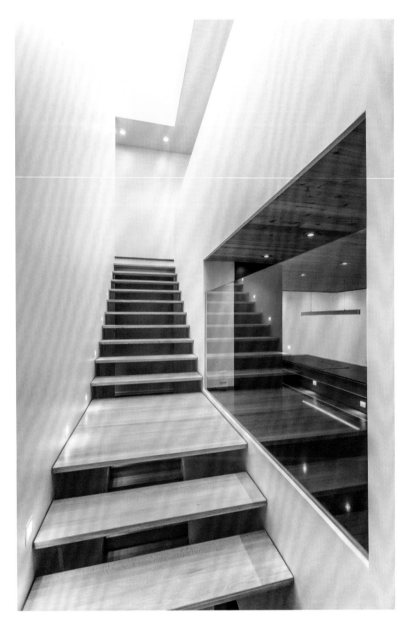

Staircase and mezzanine

Master bathroom

INDEX

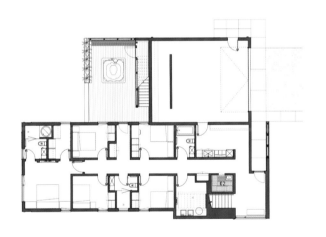 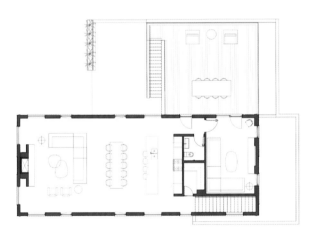

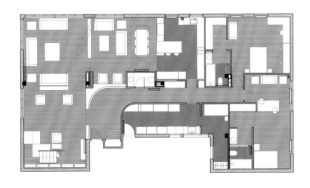 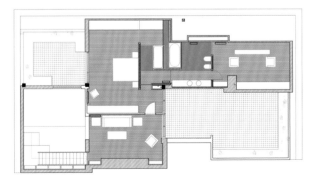

BOUNDARY P 024

Web: www.lw-id.com
Tel: +886 2 2702 2199
Email: teresa@lw-id.com

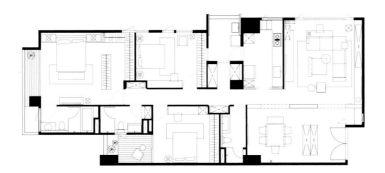

CHAMELEON P 032

Web: www.apm-mallorca.com
Tel: +34 971 69 89 00
Email: info@apm-mallorca.com

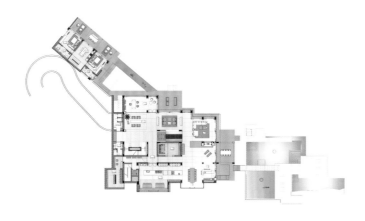

F HOUSE P 038

Web: www.onehousesh.com
Tel: +86 (21) 64226977 105
Email: lt@onehousesh.com

FLEXHOUSE P 044

Web: www.evolution-design.info
Tel: +41 44 253 9508
Email: pr@evolution-design.info

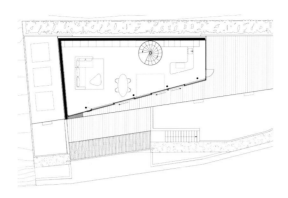

GAME—THE JOY OF LIFE COMES
FROM INFINITE EXTENSION P 052

Web: www.lw-id.com
Tel: +886 2 2702 2199
Email: teresa@lw-id.com

GRAY BOX P 058

Web: www.adcasa.hk
Tel: 0754-87122656
Email: ad87122656@163.com

HAUS BENZ P 066

Web: www.ifgroup.org
Tel: +49 711 993392-337
Email: buehling@ifgroup.org

HAUS K P 070

Web: destilat.at
Tel: +43 1 97 444 20
Email: office@destilat.at

 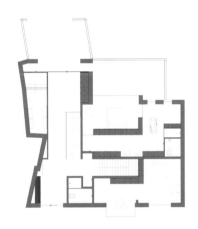 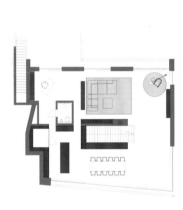

HOUSE 19 P 076

Web: a-cero.com
Tel: +34 917 997 984
Email: a-cero@a-cero.com

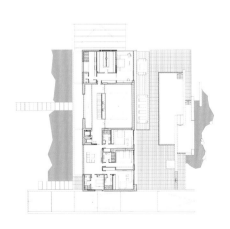 

HOUSE AN DER ACHALM P 084

Web: alexanderbrenner.de
Tel: +49 711 342436 0
Email: architekten@alexanderbrenner.de

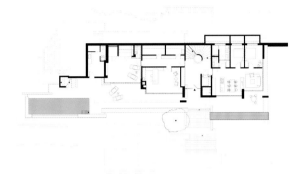
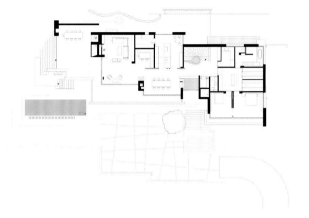

HOUSE M P 092

Web: www.monovolume.cc
Tel: +39 0471 050226
Email: patrik.pedo@monovolume.cc

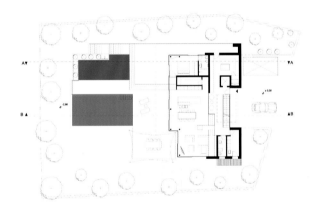

IMMERSED IN BOOKS AND GREEN P 100

Web: www.herzudesign.com
Tel: + 886 2 27316671
Email: herzudesign@gmail.com

LIGHT OF LIFE P 106

Web: www.herzudesign.com
Tel: + 886 2 27316671
Email: herzudesign@gmail.com

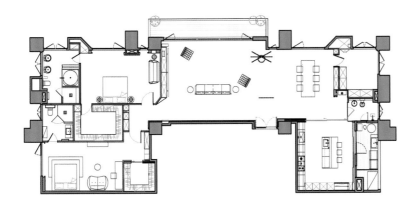

MC3 HOUSE P 114

Web: marq.cat
Tel: +34 937 243 618
Email: info@marq.cat

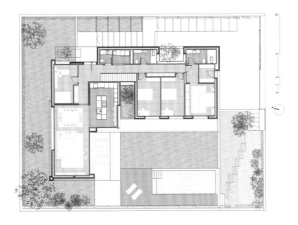

MONOLITHIC HOUSE P 122

Web: www.brainfactory.it
Tel: +39 349 4411737
Email: info@brainfactory.it

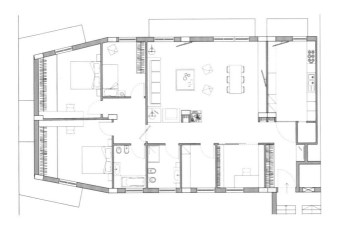

MUSICIAN'S RESIDENCE IN NAOUSA P 128

Web: www.gem-arch.gr
Tel: (210) 6838118
Email: info@gem-arch.gr

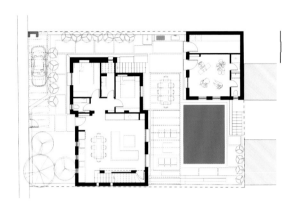 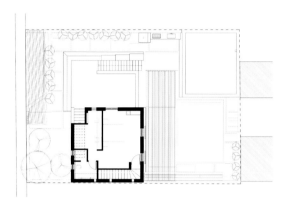

OVER WHITE P 134

Web: azovskiypahomova-architects.com
Tel: +38(098) 401 27 20
Email: juliapedan@gmail.com

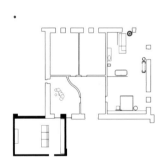 

PENTHOUSE AMSTERDAM P 140

Web: www.remymeijers.nl
Tel: +31 (0)30 2763732
Email: info@paulgeerts.nl

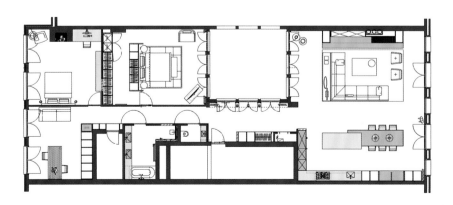

PENTHOUSE GRIFFINTOWN P 148

Web: www.mxma.ca
Tel: +1 (514) 700-4038
Email: admin@mxma.ca

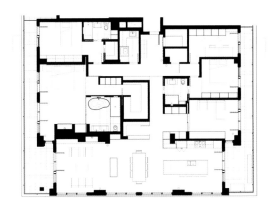

PURIFIED RESIDENCE P 156

Web: www.lw-id.com
Tel: +886 2 2702 2199
Email: teresa@lw-id.com

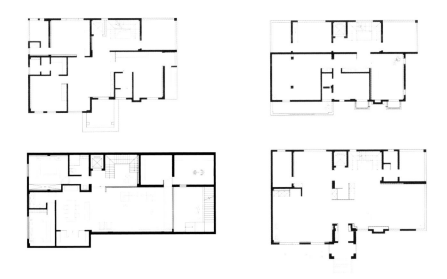

RÉSIDENCE DE L'AVENUE LAVAL P 168

Web: adhoc-architectes.com
Tel: +1 514 764 0133
Email: jf.st-onge@adhoc-architectes.com

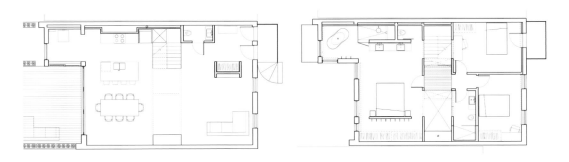

RESIDENCE OAK P 172

Web: hatem.ca
Tel: +1 418 524 1554
Email: info@hatem.ca

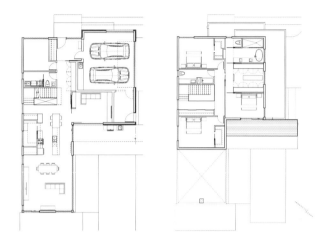

ROCA LLISA P 178

Web: www.arrcc.com
Tel: 0027 021 468 4400
Email: info@arrcc.com

SOL HOUSE P 186

Web: alexanderbrenner.de
Tel: +49 711 342436 0
Email: architekten@alexanderbrenner.de

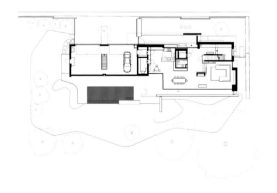

SU HOUSE P 192

Web: alexanderbrenner.de
Tel: +49 711 342436 0
Email: architekten@alexanderbrenner.de

SUITE FOR TEN P 200

Web: www.egueyseta.com
Tel: +34 931 791 992
Email: sarah@egueyseta.com

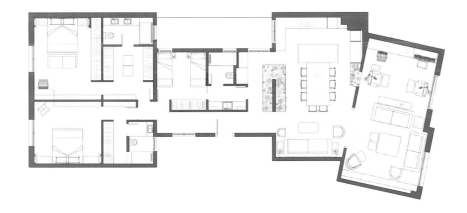

S.V. HOUSE P 208

Web: a-cero.com
Tel: +34 917 997 984
Email: a-cero@a-cero.com

THE BLACK CORE HOUSE P 220

Web: www.axelrodarchitects.com
Tel: 03 5291982
Email: info@axelrodarchitects.com

THE W.I.N.D. HOUSE P 224

Web: www.unstudio.com
Tel: +31 (0)20 570 20 40
Email: k.murphy@unstudio.com

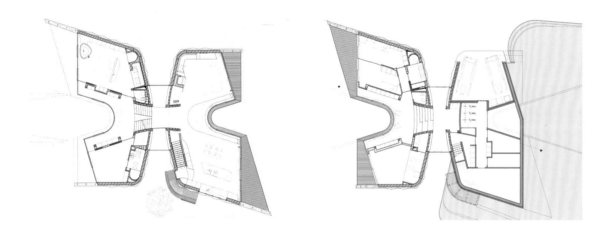

VILLA B P 232

Web: elenakarouladesign.com
Tel: +30 210 80 15 331
Email: elena@elenakarouladesign.com

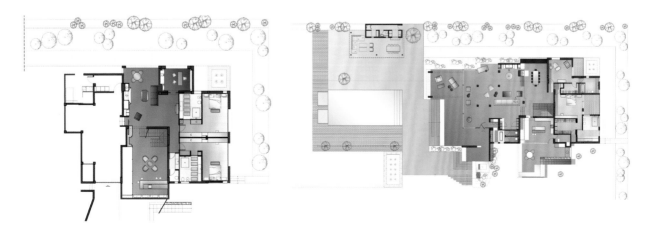

VILLA LE TRIDENT DE L'ESQUILLON P 240

Web: 4a-architekten.de
Tel: +49 711 38 93 00 0 0
Email: kontakt@4a-architekten.de

WAVERLY RESIDENCE P 246

Web: architecture-mu.com
Tel: +1 514 907 9092
Email: info@architecture-mu.com

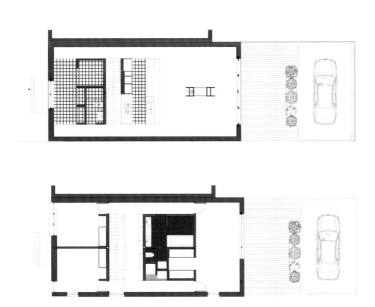

Published in Australia in 2018 by
The Images Publishing Group Pty Ltd
Shanghai Office
ABN 89 059 734 431
6 Bastow Place, Mulgrave, Victoria 3170, Australia
Tel: +61 3 9561 5544 Fax: +61 3 9561 4860
books@imagespublishing.com
www.imagespublishing.com

Copyright © The Images Publishing Group Pty Ltd 2018
The Images Publishing Group Reference Number: 1488

 A catalogue record for this
book is available from the
National Library of Australia

Title: Minimalist and Luxury Living Spaces: Fashionable Home Design
Author: Mark Rielly (Ed.)
ISBN: 9781864708011

Printed by Toppan Leefung Packaging & Printing, in Hong Kong/China

IMAGES has included on its website a page for special notices in relation to this and its other
publications. Please visit www.imagespublishing.com